The Lilies of the Field

**A Thirteen Lesson Series for
Ladies Bible Classes**

Fay Mobley

Truth
Publications

Taking His hand,
Helping each other home.
TM

ISBN 10: 1-58427-191-4

ISBN 13: 978-158427-191-8

First Printing: 2007

Truth Publications, Inc.
CEI Bookstore
220 S. Marion St., Athens, AL 35611
855-492-6657
sales@truthpublications.com
www.truthbooks.com

Foreword

The material contained in these lessons is not designed to teach anything new. God's Word is older than time itself. Sin and its consequences have not changed and God declares, "I change not." Hence, anything new would be both superfluous and ruinous.

With God's help, our aim is to "Provoke one another unto love and good works," to establish a closer relationship with God and our fellowman, and to inspire one another into greater service for the Master.

Fay Mobley

Table of Contents

The Lilies of the Field

SUGGESTIONS FOR TEACHERS

BEFORE CLASS SESSIONS:

1. Study each lesson outline carefully well in advance of the class period. Allow enough study time to:
    a. Make notes of your own comments relative to the material to be studied.
    b. Study each Scriptural reference and the context in which it is used It is often helpful to use both the King James Version and the American Standard Version.
    c. With the help of a good concordance find and make notes on additional Scriptures that are relative to the subject.
2. Plan your method of teaching and work accordingly.
    a. You may be better able to convey your thoughts by a lecture method.
    b. Perhaps you find that an informal class discussion is the best method for you.
    c. Whatever method you choose to use, it is important to allow enough time for class participation.

DURING CLASS SESSIONS:

1. Open each class period with a prayer. It is wise to get a list of those in the class who are willing to lead in prayer. From this list you may make assignments for each class period a week in advance. Do not embarrass anyone by calling upon her spontaneously. Women are not accustomed to praying publicly and they are often more reluctant to do so than men.
2. If you have one who is willing to lead the class in song, this is a good practice also.
3. Allow no more than an hour for each session.
4. Spend the first half of the class time in reviewing the lesson outline. You may wish to have students read the Scriptural references which are not quoted in the outline. The second half of the class session should be devoted to the "Exercises for Home Study and Class Discussion."
5. Encourage class participation. This makes the class far more interesting and each student feels that her contribution is important.
6. Stick to the subject under consideration. Often questions or comments are offered which tend to cause the class to stray from the subject. When this happens, kindly and tactfully direct the attention of the class back to the subject at hand.

The Young Woman: Social Pressures

ROMANS 12:2

INTRODUCTION:

Youth has risen up en masse protesting against the "Establishment." By "Establishment" they mean authority in general, whether it be in written laws or traditional scruples. Admittedly, a great deal of corruption, graft, undemocratic practices and vice exist in most "establishments" which certainly merit reformation, and perhaps peaceful protest would focus attention on these needs. However, these are not the objects of our study. We want to consider the protests against established moral rules which originated with God in Heaven. A thing is not morally right on the mere basis that it is socially accepted.

The "No God" theory is the root of many of the social ills of today, with educators playing a very prominent part. They have exalted their own knowledge above that of God and imposed upon vulnerable youth "scientific" theories which are opposed to true science and the Scriptures. Consequently, if there is no God, reasons youth, there is no one to whom man is accountable for his actions. Therefore, he may obey his every impulse and suffer no lasting consequences. Now, if he can get the "Establishment" to look upon him with favor, he is totally free to "do his thing." There is no stopping place for such sick thinking. Situation Ethics is the rule of the day. The final result is chaos, devastation and destruction even from a social standpoint, not to mention the eternal condemnation. History, both secular and Biblical, reveals the fact that every nation, without exception, engrossed in immorality, has suffered total ruin. America is not immune!

I. UNDER THE GUISE OF CONSTITUTIONAL FREEDOM, MANY ADVOCATE SUCH THINGS AS:
   A. Free love. To accomplish this so-called freedom, college students have demanded (and in many cases received) the right to live together in mixed dorms on campus. Spineless college administrators (and even some in secondary schools) have digressed into being glorified "pencil-pushers" who choose to "hear no evil, see no evil." They have allowed the wanton desires of a minority of the students to turn dorms and campuses into brothels for so-called free love. They confuse love with lustful passion and there is a vast difference. Love originated with God and is totally unselfish. It considers the needs and desires of others more than those of self. Lustful passion, on the other hand, had its inception with Satan and its sole aim is to satisfy the desires of one's own flesh.

9

B. Many want legalization of prostitution and homosexuality (Read Rom. 1:21-2:6). Legalizing sin does not make it any less sinful. The Bible strictly forbids both prostitution and homosexuality and the laws of the land can never make them morally legal.

C. The first thing Peter says one must add to his faith is virtue (2 Pet. 1:5). Virtue is simply the courage to say, "No," to Satan in whatever form he may appear. Have we that courage?

II. THERE IS NO PROBLEM FACING THE YOUNG WOMAN TODAY THAT IS NEW.

A. Because of our advanced communication system, we are more aware of youth's problems but they are not new.

　　1. The Holy Spirit inspired the apostle Paul to write these words of encouragement: "There hath no temptation taken you but such as is common to man. . ." (I Cor. 10:13).

B. Youth's problems have been intensified by centuries of humanity who have chosen to reject God's divine laws and blaspheme His name, thus perpetuating and compounding evil. "Evil men and seducers will wax worse and worse," said the apostle (2 Tim. 3:13).

C. All problems originate with humanity. Divinity has never been and is not now the author of society's ills. Rather, they come as repercussions of man's attitude toward God and / or his fellowman.

III. IT IS INEVITABLE THAT WE WILL ENCOUNTER TROUBLE IN THIS LIFE.

A. The very epitome of patience—Job himself—said, "Man that is born of woman is of few days and full of trouble" (Job 14:1). But we need not despair, for David said, "The Lord also will be a refuge for the oppressed, a refuge in times of trouble" (Psa. 9:9).

B. It is imperative that we have God as our partner in life; otherwise defeat is as certain as is trouble. One cannot fight Satan alone. There is only one force stronger than he; that is Deity.

C. Peter said, "Casting all your care (anxiety) upon him, for he careth for you" (I Peter 5:7).

　　1. One cannot cast his anxieties upon the Lord if he does not belong to Him. He will be our helper only when we obey the gospel and become a child of the Father.

D. Jesus said, "Come unto me all ye that labor and are heavy laden, and I will give you rest. Take my yoke upon you, and learn of me, for I am meek and lowly in heart: and ye shall find rest unto your souls" (Matt. 11:28-29).

1. One who is "yoked up" with Jesus has an unconquerable ally with whom he can overcome all obstacles of life. "I can do all things through Christ which strengtheneth me" said Paul (Phil. 4:13).

E. We conclude from these Scriptures that the very first thing one must do to arm himself for life's conflict is to become a Christian.

CONCLUSION:

We are fully aware of the great amount of peer pressure to which the young Christian is subjected. Amid the throng of a pleasure crazed crowd, she sometimes stands alone so far as human comradeship is concerned. However, she finds comfort in the knowledge that she is not alone for her Master has promised, "I will never leave thee, nor forsake thee" (Heb. 13:5). He, too, often stood alone and is sympathetic and compassionate (see Matt. 26:56). To stand opposed to evil is to stand approved of God (Matt. 6:24), and certainly the latter should be the most desirable position.

The young woman who clings tenaciously to her scruples (even in the midst of ridicule and persecution) is worthy of admiration and respect. More often than not her persecutors become her admirers when they see that her high moral character is unyielding. She has everything to gain and nothing to lose by standing "fast in the faith" (I Cor. 16:13). "If God be for us, who can be against us?" (Rom. 8:31).

EXERCISES FOR HOME STUDY AND CLASS DISCUSSION

1. List some theories which you believe contribute to some of the social ills of today.

    a. ———————————————————————.

    b. ———————————————————————.

    c. ———————————————————————.

2. Paul told Timothy to "——————— ——————————— lusts" (2 Tim. 2:22).

3. Name some lusts which you believe to be more common to youth.

    a. ———————————————————————.

    b. ———————————————————————.

    c. ———————————————————————.

4. Of the "Christian Graces", what is the first thing Peter lists that one must add to his faith? ——————————— (2 Pet. 1:5) Define it:

———————————————————————————————

5. List some ways in which you personally can help to revitalize Christian concepts among your peers.

a. _____.

b. _____.

c. _____.

6. What is the difference between love and lust?

a. Love is _____.

b. Lust is _____.

7. Is there any sin that is new today? Yes _____ No _____.

8. The apostle to the Hebrews states that Jesus "was in all points _____ like as we are, yet without sin" (Heb. 4:15).

9. Is it possible for such things as prostitution and homosexuality to be made legal by men? _____. Why?

10. Timothy was instructed to "Let no man despise thy _____" (I Tim. 4:12). How was he to avoid this? _____

_____.

11. Our English word, "science", comes from a Latin word which means "to know." In light of this definition, could the "No God Theory" be classified as "Scientific"? Yes _____ No _____

_____.

Why? _____-

12. Define morality: _____.

The Young Woman: Her Dress and Recreation

I TIMOTHY 2:9-10

INTRODUCTION:

To be in vogue and to enjoy a popular reputation among one's peers is the desire of most young women. In this day of the mini-skirt, short shorts, bikinis and such like, these things are frequently very real problems. The desire to be fashionable and popular is not sinful so long as one does not allow that desire to annul her knowledge of God's standard. "Everybody else is doing it" is not the rule by which the Christian is either justified or condemned. The majority is usually wrong in moral and religious matters (see Matt. 7:13-14).

What is God's standard?

I. STYLE OF DRESS.

A. In I Timothy 2:9-10, women are commanded to "adorn themselves in modest apparel, with shamefacedness and sobriety . . . with good works." Notice that this commandment is not addressed to any particular age group!

1. What is modest apparel? "Modest" simply means, "orderly, well arranged, decent." Webster also adds, "Observing the proprieties of sex." We see in the latter definition that girls who dress in boy's clothing, and vice-versa, are not dressed modestly. In the first place, it is not "adorning," and secondly, it is not proper.

2. Those who are not attempting to justify that which they know to be questionable apparel, have no difficulty understanding this Scripture. A good standard to follow is: if you question its modesty, don't wear it!

B. We are prone to emphasize "modest apparel" and ignore "with shamefacedness and sobriety," a phrase that helps us better to understand what modest apparel really is. W. E. Vine defines them thusly:

1. Shamefacedness: "Having a sense of shame." This suggests a sense of propriety that prevents an immoral act. Trench says, "An innate moral repugnance to the doing of the dishonorable act."

2. Sobriety: "Sound judgment." "It is that inner self-government with its constant rein on all the passions and desires, which would hinder the temptation to these from arising. . ." (Trench).

C. Many of today's fashions do not fit the Christian. We are told not to be fashioned according to the world (Rom. 12:2).

13

Those who are conformed to this world's evil are not transformed as is commanded. Solomon described the worldly woman in Proverbs 7:10-13 as wearing the "attire of a harlot," subtle, loud, a gadabout, stubborn, aggressive, having an "impudent face" (lacking shame).

D. Why must we dress modestly?
  1. Because God commanded it should be reason enough. However, He had a purpose for so instructing and it was not because He wanted us to appear as pious fuddy-duddies. His laws have always been for the good of mankind and this one is no exception.
  2. God dressed Adam and Eve for their good, not His own. "God cannot be tempted with evil. . .," said James (1:13).
  3. He is not a stern "kill-joy" who doesn't want us to have a good time. The opposite is true. He wants us to be happy and He knows what is necessary for our happiness.
  4. Who knows better the desires and passions of man than He who created man?
  5. The sexual desires of the human male, generally speaking, are more easily aroused than those of the female and nothing excites those passions more than the scantily clad body of a woman.

E. Jesus said the man who looks upon a woman to lust after her has committed adultery with her already in his heart (Matt. 5:28). While the man is certainly responsible for his actions, the woman who dresses in such a way as to incite his lust shares equally in his sin. And, should this lust be fulfilled, the woman will likely suffer more severe consequences.

F. It is true that some men will lust after a woman regardless of how she dresses or otherwise conducts herself. But those who have done nothing to cause this evil desire are innocent of any wrong doing and the man alone stands guilty in God's sight.

G. A classic example of "over-dressing" is the garb worn by some orders of Catholic nuns. Jesus rebuked the Scribes and Pharisees for doing things to be "seen of men" and mentions expressly "long clothing" (robes) (Mark 12:38).

H. The young Christian is always in style when she wears modest apparel. She must not appear in public in short, tight skirts, in bathing suits, etc., where men and boys are present for the reasons we have already discussed. It is possible, even probable, that she will be the object of ridicule by some. However, those persons would not make the right kinds of friends. On the other hand, if she has a good personality, is kind and considerate, is a happy, outgoing, warm individual, her peers will soon learn that her character, not her clothes, makes the girl and is the real *adornment*.

I. Our adornment must be that of a "meek and quiet spirit" (I Pet. 3:4). The outward dress must complement and reflect that inward adorning.

II. RECREATION (Re-creation).

   A. There is nothing wrong with wholesome recreation. God did not make a body that requires recreation and then condemn the requirement.

   B. Unwholesome and sinful pleasures will not re-create the body. On the contrary, they may *destroy* the body and will certainly destroy the soul. Thus, they are not truly recreation.

   C. Lasciviousness, condemned in Galatians 5:19, is described very vividly in modern dances under the guise of recreation.

      1. "Lasciviousness," while including any kind of shameful conduct, is used specifically to describe "lewd, lustful bodily movements. . .unchaste handling of male and female" (Thayer).

      2. The vulgar bodily movements of some rock performers are personifications of this word.   If this is *not* lasciviousness, then what *is* lasciviousness? Incidentally, some lyrics of rock (and country) music are vulgar, sensual and suggestive and parents should censor.

      3. Let us remember that the Bible says, "They which do such things shall not inherit the kingdom of God" (Gal. 5:21).

   D. Prolonged petting falls under the same condemnation. It is sometimes difficult for young girls to see the danger in this practice.

      1. They may truthfully say they experience no evil desires by dancing or necking. But can they *truthfully* say the same thing about the boy with whom they are engaging in these things? Once again we call your attention to the easily aroused masculine passions and once again, we emphasize the fact that the girl who causes this lust is guilty of sin.

   E. An argument may be: "Then I won't be a part of the crowd."

      1. The "crowd" to which reference is made is headed for more trouble and heartache than one can envision.

      2. Many authorities who have devoted their lives to helping Juvenile Delinquents state that most of the problems of wayward girls had their inception on the dance floor. Lust is conceived there, intensified in a parked car or other dimly lit place for necking and culminated in the act of fornication. Even if an unwanted pregnancy is not the result (which it often is), the girl is no longer pure. No decent man wants a "second-hand" woman for his bride. The boy who conquers a girl's body rarely marries that girl. If *he* can seduce her, he suspects that others could or have already done so. If he

does marry her, he feels trapped into a union which is a very poor basis for a happy marriage.

3. If you must defile your body to "hold" the boy, he is not worth holding!

4. The conscience of the boy or girl which has been trained right refuses to be subdued into indifference to right and wrong. Consequently, if only you and God know about your ugly conduct, you will not escape reproach.

5. Before you become involved in dancing, necking, mixed bathing, etc., stop and consider the consequences. Who will be hurt? You, the boy involved, your parents, his parents, your friends, God and the church. Do not allow yourself to be placed in a position wherein you might yield to temptation. Not only is your soul at stake in such cases but you are jeopardizing a lifetime of happiness.

6. God's law is: You will reap what you sow (Gal. 6:7-8; Job 4:8; Hos. 8:7). Learn from the mistakes of others and do not deceive yourself into thinking you will escape the consequences because you're smarter than Susie, or Jane, or Mary. God's law is YOU will reap what YOU sow and there are no exceptions.

CONCLUSION:

Every wise woman is concerned about her reputation and should take great care to preserve it. It takes years to build a good reputation but only a few short moments to destroy it.

There are times when the standards of men conflict with the laws of God but against decency and goodness there is no law (see Gal. 5:22-23).

EXERCISES FOR HOME STUDY AND CLASS DISCUSSION

1. The worldly woman of Proverbs 7:10-13 wears the "attire of _____."

2. The Christian who wears immodest apparel may be classified by others as "worldly". True ———— False ————.

3. Give some reasons why the Christian must be adorned in modest apparel. (See I Tim. 2:9-10; Matt. 5:28; I Pet. 3:3-5.)
   a. _____.
   b. _____.
   c. _____.

4. How does "recreation" differ from "sinful pleasure?"
   _____.

5. Define:
   a. Modesty: _____.

16

b. Shamefacedness: ———————————————

Underscore the proper answer.

1. God initiated laws for mankind for:
   a. The good of mankind.
   b. God's own veneration.
   c. To contend with civil laws.

2. Lasciviousness is:
   a. Loud, boastful jesting.
   b. Riotous living.
   c. Lewd, lustful, wanton.

3. Jesus rebuked the Scribes and Pharisees for:
   a. Keeping the law of Moses.
   b. Doing things to be "seen of men."
   c. Observing the Sabbath.

4. In Gal. 6:7-8 we learn that all mankind will:
   a. Become weary in well doing.
   b. Reap what we sow.
   c. Be overtaken in a fault.

5. Sobriety is:
   a. Sound judgment.
   b. Temperate in the use of liquor.
   c. Friendly or intimate companionship.

The Young Woman: Generation Problems

ECCLESIASTES 12:1

INTRODUCTION:

"Remember now thy creator in the days of thy youth, while the evil days come not...", said Solomon (Eccl. 12:1).

The wise man knew that the time would come when the young man or woman's mind would be pressed with problems so perplexing as to crowd out the memory of the Creator of life. Thus the admonition to remember Him in the days of youth.

The older generation is prone to look upon youth's problems as insignificant and thus are sometimes insensitive to them. Regardless of how trivial they may appear to older persons, they are very real (and often grave) to the young woman. Ignoring them will not make them "go away," nor will they be solved by such statements, as, "Forget it; when you're older it won't be important." Today's perplexities need to be untangled today. They will not need to be solved "when she is older."

I. THE GENERATION GAP.

A. As was stated in lesson number one, youth's problems are not new. There has never been a generation of youth who gave credit to the previous generation for having much understanding. The "Now" generation has never believed the "Then" generation ran world affairs wisely and they have always been convinced that they could have and would have done better.

B. Today's youth is better educated and better informed than any previous generation, and for this we are grateful. We must not, however, confuse knowledge with wisdom, and remember that youth's education and information were made possible by "old foggies" who continue to dig into history, science, mathmatics, etc., so that tomorrow's youth will excel even more in these fields.

C. Today's youth will be tomorrow's teachers, parents, diplomats, politicians, etc. whom we hope will be more understanding and sympathetic to the problems than we have been. They may not make the same mistakes we have made, and our prayer is that they won't. Nonetheless, they will make mistakes. We ask only that they apply the golden rule and treat us as they would want to be treated were they in our place.

D. I do not believe the problem is so much a matter of misun-

18

derstanding as it is of disapproval. Parents must look at both sides of the coin and try to understand the problems of their children, wisely reasoning with them. However, compromise with evil cannot be the right answer and it will compound, not solve, the problems. Youth wants to change the world—let's help them! But it must be for better and not to establish a more permissive society where inexperienced youth is free to "do his thing," liberated, so to speak, from all authority. A nation without authority would be in chaos in five minutes!!

E. "It's nobody's business what I do," is an absurd statement from one who lives in a fool's paradise. "No man is an island;" "No one lives to himself or dies to himself" (Rom. 14:7). What we do *is* somebody's business because others are inevitably affected by our actions.

II. DRUG ABUSE.

A. Drug abuse is a major world-wide problem. Many Christian parents hide their heads in the sand, so to speak, and pretend it isn't happening, or deceive themselves into thinking it will not affect their children. Nevertheless it, like all other evils, has crept into the church and reared it's ugly head in the "best" of families.

1. At the time of this writing the U.S. Supreme Court is considering the legalization of marijuana. As we have already said, "legalizing" sin does not make it any less sinful.

2. Marijuana is a mind-altering drug and it is condemned under the heading of drunkeness (Gal. 5:19; Rom. 13:13; et. al.) Needless to say, God's authority supercedes that of the U. S. Supreme Court.

a. Characteristics of drunkenness are seen in the following Scriptures: Gen. 9:20-21—irrational behavior; Gen. 19:31-35—impaired consciousness; Prov. 23:23—incoherent speech and hallucinations; Prov. 31:4-5—inability to reason. The effects of drugs are identical.

B. Time and space will not permit our going into lengthy detail on drug abuse in this lesson. Thus, we suggest that every student write the National Council on Drug Abuse, Washington, D.C. for more information on this dreadful evil.

C. Should you ever be tempted to "see what it's like," remember that there are many who never returned from their first LSD "trip." Their minds are either destroyed or irreparably impaired and the human brain is one part of the body that is incapable of reproducing healthy cells to replace those that have been destroyed (Dr. McKnight, Cincinnati Neurosurgeon).

D. There is nothing in this world more destructive than mind-altering drugs. When the mind is destroyed, the person is destroyed and there can be absolutely no hope, either mentally, physically or spiritually.

E. What possible good could come from an experience in drug abuse? Incidentally, alcohol has the same results, though its destruction is usually somewhat slower.

F. Some argue that drugs are no worse than alcohol. How does comparing one sin to another justify either? That is like saying, "I'm as good as that hypocrite?" How *good* is a hypocrite? Such statements are flimsy crutches that prove nothing!

G. Drug abuse is not peculiar to the young. Middle aged people are also pulled down to the depths of degradation by this abomination.

H. Peer pressures, insecurity, escape from reality, parents' examples, etc. are listed in various reports as causes for drug abuse. None of them are valid enough to exonerate the addict.

I. Gal. 5:20 and Rev. 21:8 condemn "sorcery" (witchcraft-KJV).
   1. The word used in the original is PHARMAKIA from which we get our English word "Pharmacy." "Primarily signified the use of medicine, drugs, spells..." (W. E. Vine).

CONCLUSION:

Dear young friend, do what is right *because* it is right, not because it is what someone else wants you to do. Never apologize for not participating in evil. Walk tall, be proud of what you are, and God will bless you with a peace that passes all understanding. Your happiness in this life and the eternal bliss of your soul depends on it.

EXERCISES FOR HOME STUDY AND CLASS DISCUSSION

1. What is the difference between knowledge and wisdom?
   a. Knowledge is ———————————————————.
   b. Wisdom   is ———————————————————.

2. Solomon said, "Remember now thy creator in the ———— ———— ———— ———— (Eccl. 12:1).

3. The "generation gap" is peculiar to this present generation. True———— False ————.

4. Give your suggestions as to how youth may help to bridge the generation gap.

————————————————————————————————

————————————————————————————————

5. Give your suggestions as to how parents and teachers may help to bridge the generation gap.

————————————————————————————————

————————————————————————————————

Underscore the correct answer or answers.

1. Rom. 13:1-7 condemns drug abuse on the basis of:
   a. Drunkenness.
   b. Illegality.
   c. Abuse of the mind.

2. The drug addict disobeys I Thess. 5:22 where God commands:
   a. "Be not drunk with wine."
   b. "Abstain from all appearance of evil."
   c. "Do not overcome evil with evil."

3. Associating with drug abusers is prohibited in
   a. I Cor. 15:33.
   b. Rom. 12:10.
   c. Rom. 12:18.

4. Drug addicts use drugs to
   a. Correct an imbalance of body chemistry.
   b. Escape reality.
   c. Alter the emotions.

5. Parents can better understand and help one another by applying
   a. Eph. 6:1-4 and Col. 3:10-21.
   b. Gal. 5:19-21.
   c. Prov. 1:7-9.

The Wife: A Help Meet for Man
GENESIS 2:18-24

INTRODUCTION:

Solomon said, "Whose findeth a wife findeth a good thing. . ." (Prov. 18:22). The idea, of course, expressed in this proverb is that those who find a *good* wife find a good thing. The same wise king also said, "It is better to dwell in the wilderness, than with a contentious and an angry woman" (Prov. 21:19); and "It is better to dwell in a corner of the housetop, than with a brawling woman in a wide house (Prov. 21:9).

Our lesson is centered on how we may be the good wife of Proverbs 18 and avoid being the kind described in Proverbs 21.

I. HER CREATION AND PURPOSE.

A. "And the Lord God said, it is not good that man should be alone; I will make him an help meet for him." Notice the wording of this passage (Gen. 2:18). At first glance it looks as though there is a grammatical error; too many "hims" in the sentence. Such is not the case but rather God was to make *of* Adam a help meet *for* Adam. That is, He would make a part of Adam into a help meet for him. Please note that Eve was a wife when she was created.

　1. "Help meet" is often misquoted as "helpmate." Whereas the right kind of wife is both a help and a mate to her husband, the two words, "help meet" have a much richer meaning.

B. Adam had all of God's creation at his beck and call, so to speak, and yet God said he was alone. "There was not found an help meet for him" (Gen. 2:20).

　1. The Biblical connotation of the word "meet" is: Fitting, worthy, proper. For example: John the Baptist told those Jews who came to him to be baptized, "Bring forth therefore fruits *meet* for repentance" (Matt. 3:8).

　2. Thus, we see that woman was the only creature in all of God's creation that fit man's needs and was a worthy help for him.

C. God did not choose to produce woman from the dust as He did Adam. I believe this is significant. We may not know all the reasons for this but we can be sure that He had a purpose in so choosing. He certainly had the power to form her from the dust.

　1. God said husband and wife were to be "one flesh," showing the unity of man and woman. Is not this unity demonstrated

in the act of forming woman from the rib of man? "This is now bone of my bones, and flesh of my flesh...", said Adam (Gen. 2:23).

2. One ancient philosopher wrote: "She was made of a rib taken from his side, not made out of his head, to rule over him; nor out of his feet, to be trampled upon, but out of his side, to be equal with him; under his arm, to be protected; and near his heart, to be loved." This is a very accurate description of her position.

3. They are indeed two personalities but should be "one flesh" in the same way that the Father and Son are one. "I and my Father are one" (Jno 10:30). That is, they are one in purpose, will and work and they are inseparable.

D. I believe the phrase, "one flesh," is used both literally and metaphorically.

1. In I Cor. 6:16 Paul teaches that man and woman become "one flesh" in the sexual union.

   a. God's law is that they become "one flesh." Accordingly, we learn from a study of I Cor. 7:1-5 that neither marriage partner has "power" over his or her body. That is, neither have the right (except by mutual consent "for a time"-verse 5) to refrain from sexual union with their spouse.

2. When man and woman produce an offspring, that child is one flesh literally and is the combination of both parents. That man and woman physically became one flesh both in the conception and in the "product" needs no clarification.

E. How may we apply and understand the metaphor?

1. It was unnecessary that God teach Adam and Eve to love one another. Eve was as much a part of Adam as was his physical heart.

2. The law of self-preservation is perhaps one of the strongest urges in the world. By instinct, we protect our own bodies from hurt or harm. Paul, in comparing the love of a man for his wife with that of Christ for the church, said, "So ought men to love their wives as their own bodies. He that loveth his wife loveth himself. For no man ever yet hated his own flesh; but nourisheth and cherisheth it, even as the Lord the church" (Eph. 5:28-29).

3. We necessarily conclude that if husbands are to love their wives as their own bodies, then wives are to love their husbands in the very same way. Should we apply this Scripture to ourselves, what would our attitudes be toward our husbands?

   a. Although our legal system makes the husband responsible for the debts of his wife, would we make purchases for which our husbands find it difficult to pay? Would we ridicule or slander them? Would we nag at them until their nerves were frayed? Would we try to make them over? Or—

    b. Would we, with our husband's approval, buy only that which the budget allows, praise their good qualities, help them realize their goals, accept them as they are, etc.?

4. Let us remember that God said we are "one flesh" and gratefully conduct our lives to complement this great blessing.

II. HOW MAY THE WIFE BEST SERVE THE PURPOSE FOR WHICH SHE WAS CREATED?

A. Woman was created equal with man in level of importance, Women's Lib to the contrary notwithstanding, but the sphere in which she is to move is different. She is not to lead man.

1. We need only read one chapter in the Bible to see the disastrous results of woman in the role of leader, namely, Genesis three.

2. The serpent was "more subtle (cunning) than any beast of the field which the Lord God had made" (Gen. 3:1). He obviously knew that his appeal would be more readily received by the woman and thus his planned deception found favor with Eve.

3. The apostle Paul said, "Adam was not deceived, but the woman being deceived was in the transgression" (I Tim. 2:14).

4. Notice that he did not say Adam did not sin, but rather that he "was not *deceived.*" Adam knew exactly what he was doing and yet he followed the lead of his wife. Both suffered the consequences of which they had been warned. Incidentally, there is no indication that Eve had to beg Adam to transgress God's law, or that he offered any argument at all. This is a classic example of the incomparable feminine influence over the masculine mind wherein Satan's purpose is so often served.

CONCLUSION:

A careful study of Proverbs 31 will reveal a very clear picture of the kind of wife each of us should strive to be. Solomon said such a wife is a "good thing," and that her price is "far above rubies."

EXERCISES FOR HOME STUDY AND CLASS DISCUSSION

1. God formed woman from the ————— of man (Gen. 2:21-22).

2. Why was it unnecessary that Adam be taught to love his wife? (Gen. 2:23)

3. In what way does the law of self-preservation depict man's concern for his wife (Eph. 5:28-29)?

_____.

4. How may the phrase "one flesh" be seen literally? _____

_____.

Metaphorically? _____

_____.

5. In I Tim. 2:14, Paul said, "Adam was not _____, but the _____ being deceived was in the transgression."

Underscore the correct answer.

1. The wife is said to be a _____ for man (Gen. 2:18).
   a. Helpmate
   b. Blessing
   c. Help meet

2. The word "meet" as used in Genesis 2 means
   a. To encounter a friend
   b. Fitting, worthy, proper
   c. To make a new acquaintance

3. The husband is to love his wife as
   a. His own body
   b. His mother and father
   c. Christ loved the church

4. In speaking of the transgression of Adam and Eve (I Tim. 2:14), Paul said Adam
   a. Was approached by Satan
   b. Was not deceived
   c. Was exonerated from guilt

5. In Prov. 21:9 Solomon said, rather than live with a brawling woman it is better
   a. "Not to marry"
   b. "To dwell in a corner of the housetop"
   c. "To dwell in the wilderness"

The Wife:
Her Subjection and Responsibilities

EPHESIANS 5:22-23

INTRODUCTION:

Being the wife of the man we love is a very great blessing. Every wife should be determined to enjoy this reputation: "She will do him good and not evil all the days of her life;" and "She looketh well to the ways of her household, and eateth not the bread of idleness (Prov. 31:12, 27).

I. THE SUBJECTION OF THE WIFE.

    A. Once we learn and accept the fact that woman's place is one of subjection and not of authority, we will be well on our way to being the proverbial "worthy woman."

    B. Many dislike the word subjection: perhaps one of the reasons being that its meaning is obscure or completely misunderstood. The Bible defines it for us.

        1. In Rom. 8:7, the apostle stated: ". . .the carnal mind is enmity against God; for it is not *subject* to the law of God, neither indeed can be." Does he mean that the law of God does not *apply* to the carnal (evil) mind? No, he is simply saying that the carnal mind is in opposition to rather than compatible with His law. Carnality and righteousness are opposites and thus the carnal mind, so long as it remains carnal, will not submit to the authority of God.

        2. Again, in Romans 13:1, the Holy Spirit commands: "Let every soul be *subject* unto the higher powers," that is, the civil authorities. Does this mean we are slaves, owned by the civil government? Again the answer is obviously, "No." We are blessed by the laws of the land; protected by them, not enslaved by them. We are free to live as we choose so long as our actions do not conflict with civil statutes. Surely no one would be so foolish as to think we could survive without being subject to authority. Obedience to Divine law is predicated upon our being in subjection to the laws of the land and to our husbands.

        3. The woman who is wise enough to choose a husband who is a true servant of Christ will have no difficulty subjecting herself to him. He will not make unreasonable demands upon her but will consider her well-being unselfishly. No wife, however, has the prerogative of submitting to the will of a husband whose demands conflict with God's law (see Acts 5:29). This is the one and only area wherein God has restricted the authority of the

husband. The man who loves his wife as Christ loved the church will "give honor unto the wife as unto the weaker (not inferior) vessel" (I Pet. 3:7).

    C. "Wives, submit yourselves unto your own husbands, as unto the Lord. For the husband is the head of the wife, even as Christ is the head of the church. . ." (Eph. 5:22-23).

       1. Husbands have not the right to delegate their authority to their wives and wives must not accept it. God gave the authority to the man and He did not give him permission to "pass it on."

         a. This does not mean that the wife has no responsibility to make decisions. It is very often necessary for her to make decisions and act upon them. She is not free, however, to make decisions, however large or small, in opposition to her husband's wishes.

       2. Some wives think they are better equipped to be the head than are their husbands. That does not alter God's plan at all. His wisdom is far superior to ours and we should accept it without lament.

II. THE WIFE MUST CONDUCT HER LIFE SO AS TO DESERVE RESPECT.

    A. Respect is not a gift, it is something we earn. Those who have no self-respect need not expect it from others. It is essential that we live clean, godly lives if we are to gain this wonderful attribute.

       1. Peter tells us to adorn ourselves with a "meek and quiet spirit" (I Pet. 3:4), and God also gives us instructions for our outward adorning (I Tim. 2:9-10).

       2. Our speech must be "seasoned with salt" (Col. 4:6). "A soft answer turneth away wrath" (Prov. 15:1).

       3. Women should cultivate the kind, delicate speech which demonstrates her femininity. She has long been the object of jesting when the tongue is involved and regretfully, in many cases, justifiably.

       4. Some of us do a lot of talking without saying anything. This is a very detrimental characteristic which neither man nor woman appreciates. The man whose wife is a "chatterbox" has a hindrance rather than a help.

III. THE WIFE MUST BE A HOMEMAKER.

    A. Marriage and housework go together. When we marry the man of our choice, we automatically accept the responsibility of making a home for him and for the family we hope to have.

    B. Although being a good housekeeper is a part of being a homemaker, it is only a part. The cleanest house in the neighborhood is not necessarily the best home. Certainly filth is unacceptable—it manifests slothfulness (see Rom.

12:11) and is in no way compatible with Christianity. A lazy, dirty woman is offensive to nearly everyone.

C. On the other hand, some women are so obsessed with keeping a spotless house that they haven't time to keep a home. They will not invite others into their homes unless they have hours, or days, to "clean." And—if they do extend an invitation, their guests are ill at ease lest they disturb something in the immaculate surroundings. This is not conducive to practicing hospitality.

D. We must be good housekeepers, but not obsessed with it; thifty shoppers, but not to the extent of doing without the things our family needs; hospitable and charitable, etc.

E. The happy homemaker is the one who takes pride in her work, knowing that she is serving herself, her family, and God in this capacity. Housework is drudgery only to those who care little for the comforts of their families.

F. Whereas material possessions are necessary for our livelihood, they contribute little toward making a house a home. Our aim is not to "keep up with the Jones' with "things," but rather to make a warm, happy haven for ourselves and our families.

IV. THE WIFE MUST NOT BE JEALOUS, NAGGING OR CONTENTIOUS.

A. The jealous wife is demonstrating her distrust in her husband. Such actions can have very serious repercussions. Trust is one of the elements for a happy marriage and it must continue if the marriage is to survive.

1. Jealousy is not aimed exclusively at the husband's affection for other woman. One can be (and often is) jealous of her husband's time, talents, etc., none of which contribute to harmony and happiness.

B. The nagging, contentious wife is best described by Solomon in Proverbs 27:15: "A continual dripping in a very rainy day and a contentious woman are alike." Needless to say, there is little virtue in such women. A dripping faucet in the house is a constant source of agitation. So it is with a contentious wife.

CONCLUSION:

We know of no better way to summarize this lesson than is found in the words of Solomon in Proverbs 31:10-12: "Who can find a virtuous woman? For her price is far above rubies. The heart of her husband doth safely trust in her, so that he shall have no lack of gain. She will do him good and not evil all the days of his life." "Favour is deceitful, and beauty is vain; but a woman that feareth the Lord, she shall be praised" (Proverbs 31:30).

According to I Kings 11:3, Solomon had 300 wives and 700 concubines. Who would be in a better position to analyze and instruct wives than this great king? Yet he allowed his wives to turn away his heart (I Kings 11:3). No normal man is immune to feminine charms and influence. Let us make sure ours are aimed in the right direction.

EXERCISES FOR HOME STUDY AND CLASS DISCUSSION

1. Define *subjection:* _____
   _____.
2. God has placed one restriction upon man's authority over his wife. What is it? _____.
3. If women were better equipped for leadership than man, would God not have authorized that she be the head of the husband? _____
4. Peter said wives must be adorned with a "_____ and _____ spirit" (I Pet. 3:4).
5. Name some specific ways in which I Peter 3:4 may be applied.
   a. _____
   b. _____
   _____
6. Define *adorn:* _____
7. Are the terms "homemaker" and "housekeeper" completely synonymous? _____
   What is the difference? _____
8. How does Romans 12:11 apply to the homemaker?
   _____
9. By what Scripture(s) or Biblical principle is a poor housekeeper either condemned or justified? _____
10. "Favor is _____ and beauty is _____: but a woman that feareth the Lord, she shall be praised" (Prov. 31:30).
11. Jealousy is a demonstration of one's lack of _____ in her husband.
12. The nagging wife is compared to a "_____ _____ in a very rainy day" (Prov. 27:15).
13. Solomon's wives turned his heart from the Lord (I Kings 11). How did they accomplish this? _____
14. List some "Do's" and "Dont's" for the good wife.

DO	DON'T
_____	_____
_____	_____
_____	_____

The Mother
PROVERBS 31:28

INTRODUCTION:

"Mother" is one of the sweetest words in our language. The importance of being a mother cannot be exaggerated. Someone has said, "The hand that rocks the cradle rules the world." The influence and teachings of mother is a great legacy upon which men who rule lean heavily. Abraham Lincoln said, "All that I am, or ever hope to be I owe to my mother." A mother was the only human parent our Saviour had.

There is much more to being a mother than merely possessing the ability to bear children. This physical act makes one a parent in the eyes of the world but God requires much more.

Our children are gifts from God and they are to be loved and cherished, cared for and taught. The Psalmist said, "Lo, children are an heritage of the Lord and the fruit of the womb is his reward" (Psa. 127:3).

I. THE VOCATION OF MOTHERHOOD.

A. Ask any little girl what she wants to be when she grows up and almost invariably she will say, "I want to be a mommy." This is a very great compliment to the mother of that child.

B. Motherhood is indeed a vocation; a business; a career—but it differs in so many ways from other businesses. The "Product" cannot be compared to anything else in the world.

C Mother is a cook, a nurse, a laundress, a counsellor, a teacher, a housekeeper, an economist, an accountant and much, much more—she is a "Mommy."

D. I wouldn't trade the words, "I love you, mommy," for all the treasures the world has to offer. The feeling a mother gets upon hearing those words from the lips of her child is the best definition I know for "Mother." Our son and daughter are now adults with families of their own. Quite frequently we have the opportunity to talk with them by phone and the conversation nearly always ends with, "I love you, mom." Those words are just as dear and precious to me now as they were over two decades ago.

E. There is no vocation, for which woman may aspire, that is worthy to be compared with that of being a good mother.

II. THE EXAMPLE OF MOTHER.

A. Although we teach our children in many ways, example is by far the most effective.

B. As it is with any endeavor, our primary step in preparing for motherhood is to be a Christian. Unless Christ is the basis of our strength, we have a very shaky foundation upon which to build the character of our children. They must not only hear about God, they must *see* Him in us.

C. We are commanded to bring up our children in the "nurture and admonition of the Lord" (Eph. 6:4). "Train up a child in the way he should go; and when he is old, he will not depart from it" (Prov. 22:6).

D. Of Jesus, Luke said, "He began both to do and to teach" (Acts 1:11). We must first *do*, then our *words* of teaching will have the desired effect. A "do as I say, not as I do" will accomplish very little.

E. Some wonder at what age children should begin to be taught. We are reminded of a noted phychologist who was speaking on the subject of training children when the mother of a five year old boy asked, "When should I start training my son?" "Hurry home," was the answer, "You have already wasted five of the most important years of his life."

F. Even a tiny infant senses the moods of the mother. Have you ever noticed that your baby is more restless and fretful when you are not feeling well or are disturbed about something?

　　a. Whereas it is impossible for mother to always be happy and cheerful, a very good motto is found in Phil. 4:6-7: "In nothing be anxious: but in everything by prayer and supplication, let your requests be made known unto God. And the peace of God, which passeth all understanding, shall keep your hearts and minds through Christ Jesus." Never borrow trouble from tomorrow. "Sufficient unto the day is the evil thereof" (Matt. 6:34b). Time is too valuable for mother to waste any of it in needless worry.

G. *Sending* your child to the services of the church will accomplish little. We recently saw a cartoon in a church bulletin depicting a small boy who was being sent to Sunday school against his wishes. His father was in bed and the little boy was asking, "Daddy, did you go to Sunday school when you were little?" "Yes," replied his father, "every Sunday." The little boy responded with this statement: "Well, I bet it won't do *me* any good either." *Take* your child to the services of the church.

III. PROVIDING RECREATION.

A. Some bemoan the fact that the church does not provide enough recreation for the young people. Need we be reminded that the church is a spiritual institution and she is not in the recreation business?

B. It is true that the young people in the church need to socialize with one another, but it is the duty of the home, not the church, to provide recreation.

C. There are some types of recreation in which the Christian cannot participate with God's sanction. On the other hand everyone, especially young people need social activities. Let us not think the sordid activities of a few labels all young people as bad.

D. "All work and no play" does indeed make "Jack a dull boy." Thus, parents must open their homes to the friends of their children for parties and get-togethers. As with any useful endeavor, both time and effort are involved in this aspect of the child's training. If soda pop is too expensive, serve Kool-Aid. If you cannot afford to buy hot dogs, a lot of popcorn can be bought for pennies. But, by all means, provide the right kind of recreation.

E. If parents do not raise their children in the way they should go, all the collective projects in the world will not save the children.

F. Let your children know that the home belongs to them as surely as it belongs to you.

CONCLUSION:

The job of motherhood is a tremendous task but the blessings are overwhelming. Let us keep the line of communication ever open between God and ourselves as well as that between our children and ourselves. The right combination of love, prayer and work is a recipe that makes mother into the kind whose children can truly, "Rise up and call her blessed" (Prov. 31:28). Excepting the gift of God's Son, no greater blessing has ever been bestowed upon woman than that of being a good mother.

EXERCISES FOR HOME STUDY AND CLASS DISCUSSION

1. What is the most effective method of teaching children? ⸺

2. We are commanded to bring up our children in the "⸺ and ⸺ of the Lord" (Eph. 6:4).

3. Luke said Jesus "began both to ⸺ and to ⸺ " (Acts 1:1). Is the order in which Jesus' activities here are mentioned of any significance? ⸺

4. With whom should one begin to apply Romans 12:17? ⸺

5. "Actions speak louder than words" is a truism. List some specific areas where it is applicable in spiritual training of children.

   a. _____

   b. _____

   c. _____

6. What does Phil. 4:6-7 mean to you personally? ————————

7. What is one valuable lesson a mother can learn from Hebrews 12:6? ————————————————————
   ————————————————————————————

8. Define *nurture:* ————————————————————
   ————————————————————————————

9. Define *admonition:* ————————————————————
   ————————————————————————————

10. David said our children are an "———— of the Lord" (Psa. 127:3).

The Training of Children
PROVERBS 22:6

INTRODUCTION:

"And Jesus increased in wisdom and stature, and in favor with God and man" (Luke 2:52). This Scripture shows the intellectual, physical, spiritual and social growth of the Lord. Parental responsibility to train their children in all facets of life is seen in this passage.

I. THE PHYSICAL CARE AND GROWTH.

    A. Of necessity, the first concern of the mother for her baby is for his physical well being. He is helpless and in need of loving care.

        1. This is a very important part of being a mother and cannot be overemphasized. Most of us spend a great deal of time and energy seeing that our babies are kept clean, well fed, etc., and rightly so.

        2. In so doing we are not only caring for their physical needs, but at the same time we are teaching them that their well being is important to us. Few mothers stand in need of extensive teaching in this area. It seems to be inherent in women to possess this quality. (There are exceptions, of course.)

II. THE INTELLECTUAL GROWTH OF OUR CHILDREN IS OF MAJOR CONCERN ALSO.

    A. A mental dwarf is a very pitiable creature.

        1. This growth does not begin in the school room; it begins in the nursery. It is usually the mother who introduces the child to the beauties of life. A child's mind is completely open and constantly receptive to learning about new things.

        2. I have never known a normal little child who did not pick a bouquet of flowers for mommy. It is often made up of dandelions, goldenrod and chiggerweed but it demonstrates the child's appreciation for the beautiful things of nature. This appreciation should be stimulated, never curbed. This is an excellent oportunity to teach the child about the One who created the beautiful flowers.

    B. The child who is taught early in life that there are no short cuts to knowledge will not cheat in the class room or wherever he is. Honesty is never out of place. To "provide things honest in the sight of all men" (Rom. 12:17), one must begin with self.

    C. Knowledge does not come by a miracle, nor is it a gift. It is something we acquire by our own efforts. It is much easier for mother to impart knowledge than it is to instill in the learner the *desire* for knowledge. The wise mother recognizes this truth and begins very early in the life of her child to stimulate his interest in learning.

III. SOCIAL TRAINING.

A. Every normal human being wants and needs social acceptance. Jesus grew "in favor with God *and man.*"

1. The child who is favorably accepted socially has been taught that he or she must contribute something to society. It has often been said, "If you want friends, you must be one."

B. The world already has all the social parasites it can use (and then some)! Those who think the world owes them something while they contribute nothing should be rudely awakened when they try to collect. This kind of "worm" is the product of many things, not the least of which is that they haven't been taught responsibility. We must teach our children that the world owes us nothing we have not earned and that includes respect and dignity.

1. Giving a child everything he wants with no contribution from him is the best way I know to develop a social reject such as we have been discussing. He soon learns to expect everything and appreciate nothing.

2. The mother who has not taught her child, both by her words and actions that he has a responsibility to his fellowman, and that the rights of others are to be respected, has failed miserably!

IV. DISCIPLINE IS A VERY IMPORTANT PART OF TRAINING.

A. Harsh, unjust discipline is as bad, if not worse, than none at all.

B. Some years ago, I heard a mother say of her four year old daughter (who was at the time displaying a temper tantrum), "I love her too much to spank her."

1. Surely no one would say that God doesn't love his children and yet the Hebrew apostle said, "For whom the Lord loveth he chasteneth, and scourgeth every son whom he receiveth. If ye endure chastening, God dealeth with you as with sons; for what son is he whom the father chasteneth not?" (Heb. 12:6). The words of Solomon recorded in Prov. 13:24 reads: "He that spareth his rod hateth his son: but he that loveth him chasteneth him betimes."

C. There are two kinds of discipline—instructive and corrective, both of which are very important and neither of which is easy.

D. No two children are alike and each requires his or her own most effective discipline; but all require some kind.

E. Let us make sure we have properly instructed—then properly correct. Let the punishment fit the "crime." The threat: "Just wait until your daddy gets home" is cowardly and turns daddy into something the child dreads rather than welcomes.

V. MOTHERS MUST BE IMPARTIAL.

A. We sometimes hear women say, "He (or she) is my favorite child." How sad!

B. All of us have known children who were favorites and also those who were not. We do not know which to pity most. "Mother's little darling" who can do nothing wrong is usually spoiled to the extent that he or she is a nuisance. Nevertheless we pity them because we know they will likely have few friends and much unhappiness in life. On the other hand, the thwarted child is often an introvert, many times rebellious, insecure, and feels that he can do nothing right. An object of pity indeed!

C. Each child is an individual with his or her own peculiarities. Trying to fashion him into a carbon copy of someone else is doing him a very grave injustice.

D. A child should never be compared to Sam or John or Mary or Kathy. "Why can't you be more like your sister" is neither instructive nor constructive, but destructive.

E. Some children need more help from parents than others. Some learn more slowly, some are "all thumbs," etc. That does not give us license to ignore the others.

F. It takes a great deal of wisdom and patience to deal with the particular needs of each child individually. No mother is perfect and all will make errors. We need not be afraid to apologize to our children. On the contrary, they need to know that we are human, subject to mistakes the same as they. Children are quick to forgive and forget. Unfortunately, we tend to lose this wonderful characteristic somewhere along the road to adulthood.

CONCLUSION:

"Train up a child in the way he should go: and when is is old, he will not depart from it" (Prov. 22:6).

EXERCISES FOR HOME STUDY AND CLASS DISCUSSION

1. At what age should children begin to be taught? ———————

2. List some ways wherein one can stimulate the child's desire to learn.

   a. ————————————————————————

   b. ————————————————————————

   c. ————————————————————————

   d. ————————————————————————

3. How does one acquire knowledge? ———————————

4. What Scripture tells of the intellectual, physical, spiritual and social growth of our Lord? ⸺⸺⸺⸺⸺

5. In what four areas must a child grow if he is to reach complete maturity?

⸻⸻⸻⸻⸻   ⸻⸻⸻⸻⸻

⸻⸻⸻⸻⸻   ⸻⸻⸻⸻⸻

6. There are two kinds of discipline. Name them.

⸻⸻⸻⸻⸻   ⸻⸻⸻⸻⸻

7. In what order should the discipline of question number six be administered? First ⸻⸻⸻⸻⸻⸻, then ⸻⸻⸻⸻
⸻⸻⸻⸻.

8. It is the duty of the ⸻⸻⸻ to provide recreation.

9. List some childish characteristics that should be stimulated.

⸻⸻⸻⸻⸻   ⸻⸻⸻⸻⸻

⸻⸻⸻⸻⸻   ⸻⸻⸻⸻⸻

⸻⸻⸻⸻⸻   ⸻⸻⸻⸻⸻

10. List some childish characteristics that should be patiently curbed.

⸻⸻⸻⸻⸻   ⸻⸻⸻⸻⸻

⸻⸻⸻⸻⸻   ⸻⸻⸻⸻⸻

⸻⸻⸻⸻⸻   ⸻⸻⸻⸻⸻

The Church Worker:
Her Talents and Knowledge
PHILIPPIANS 2:12

INTRODUCTION:

Those who have set their goal on enjoying the pleasures of heaven recognize the fact that there is much work to do in this life. No one will get to heaven by accident.

There are two very dangerous extremes that the worker must avoid. First, the one wherein a great deal of zeal is possessed but "not according to knowledge" (see Romans 10:2). This extreme is exemplified by the person who wades into deep water before she realizes that she can not swim! Secondly, there is the person who is so afraid of doing something wrong that she does not do anything at all. Between these two extremes are the workers with whom God is pleased.

We believe this cliche' rings true: Opportunity plus ability equals responsibility.

I. **THE WORKER'S TALENTS** (Matthew 25:14-30).

A. Our Lord did much of His teaching in parables. He recognized the fact that finite minds could better comprehend the spiritual lesson by a comparison with the physical or material.

B. We understand that the talents referred to in Matt. 25 were literally money. (A gold talent was the equivalent of about $26,380 in American money; a silver talent slightly less.) Nonetheless, the lesson to be learned is:

1. The Lord gives to everyone that which he or she can best use according to this several ability—verse 15.
2. He requires that we use what He has given us. We either use or lose our talents.
3. There will be a day of reckoning.
4. The destiny of both the profitable and unprofitable servants is clearly seen in this parable.

C. Talents are nearly as diversified as are people. Many of us possess the same talents but few to the same degree. For example: most of us can cook but we all know those who excel in this art. We can all *follow* a recipe, but the very talented can *design* the recipe, etc. We have heard of many artists who nearly starved because, try as they might, they did not possess the talent to be great in that field. Of course, even the great artists did not become great by hiding their talents; they had to develop them.

D. We must first recognize what our talent or talents are (and we all have at least one), then work to develop them.

E. The apostle Paul very vividly explains the role of each Christian in I Corinthians 12:13-17 by comparing the body of Christ to the physical body. Each has his or her own responsibility and the "eye" cannot do the work of the "ear," etc. Incidentally, there is not one insignificant member in the body nor is one member superior to another. It is as foolish for one Christian to be jealous of another's work or talent as it would be for our hands to be jealous of our feet!

F. This Scripture also stresses the care we must have for those who are weak and heretofore have not performed their function. All our attention is focused upon a member of our physical body that is weak, sick, injured, etc., and we work long and hard to restore it to its proper place. So it should be with a weak member of the Lord's body. (See Gal. 6:1-2; Rom. 15:1.)

G. The day will come when we must give account to the Lord as to how we used our talents. Even when we have done all we can, we will still be in need of much of His grace and mercy to balance the ledger. What, then will be the outcome of those who have done nothing?

II. THE WORKER'S KNOWLEDGE (2 Peter 1:5).

A. Ignorance is one of Satan's most effective tools. It is as old as time itself and will continue as long as time remains. Ignorance breeds ignorance and thus it is self-propagating. Ignorance is sad in any field, but ignorance of God's word is disastrous. As it was with the Jews whom Paul described in Romans 10, so it is with us. When we are "ignorant of God's righteousness," we "go about to establish our own righteousness." There is no such thing as righteousness unless it is of God. The so-called righteousness which man concocts avails nothing (Titus 3:5; Eph. 2:8-9).

B. Knowledge of God's word is not optional—it is commanded(2 Peter 3:18). Once again we stress the fact that there are no short cuts to knowledge and, unlike talents, it is not a gift of God. Rather, we gain knowledge by our own efforts; namely study. There is no more a substitute for knowledge than there is for faith. . .lack of either will condemn us.

C. We concede that portions of the Bible are difficult to understand and we may never, in this life, understand it all. However, the Lord did not give us a law of pardon that we cannot understand. Those who use the excuse, "I can't understand the Bible" will not escape the consequences of failing to add knowledge to their faith and virtue.

D. It is a well known axiom that one cannot believe in something about which he has not heard. "How shall they believe in him of whom they have not heard?" (Rom. 10:14). "Faith cometh by hearing, and hearing by the word of God" (Rom. 10:17). This faith is not confined to the plan of salvation but includes all the word of God. One can hear, believe, repent, confess and be baptized and be lost, if he fails to grow as is required.

E. Whereas it is true that knowledge comes only by study, there are many ways we can study effectively. Study our Bibles in our homes, purchase good reference books, learn the use of words, give undivided attention to Bible teachers and preachers (always comparing their teachings with the Bible), attend home Bible classes. . .to mention a few. The Bible is the richest book in the world and is the only book, the contents of which will not be destroyed either *by* the world or *with* the world (See I Peter 1:23; Matthew 24:35).

CONCLUSION:

"Study (give diligence) to show thyself approved unto God, a workman that needeth not to be ashamed, rightly dividing the word of truth" (2 Tim. 2:15). "All scripture is given by inspiration of God, and is profitable for doctrine, for reproof, for correction, for instruction in righteousness: that the man of God may be perfect (complete), thoroughly furnished unto all good works" (2 Tim. 3:16-17).

EXERCISES FOR HOME STUDY AND CLASS DISCUSSION

1. What is a parable? ——————————————————

———————————————————————————————

2. Why did Jesus choose to do much of His teaching by using parables? ————————————————————

———————————————————————————————

3. We learn from the parable found in Matt. 25:14-30 that every accountable being has at least ———— talent.

4. In what way may an unused talent be compared to an unused muscle in the body? ————————————————

5. ———————— is one of Satan's most effective tools.

6. For one to grow in grace he must also grow in ———————— (see 2 Pet. 3:18).

7. Some use the old adage: "Little known, little required," How

does this conflict with Bible teaching? (See 2 Pet. 3:18; John 6:44-45; Phil. 2:12; Jas. 2:24.)

_____

8. The Jews by their ignorance, had gone about to establish _____ _____ _____ (Rom. 10:2).

9. All that one need do to be eternally saved is to believe, repent, confess and be baptized. True _____ false _____.

10. What are the two extremes the church worker must avoid?

_____   _____

11. Study I Cor. 12:13-27 and then list some ways in which the spiritual body may be compared to the physical body.

_____   _____

_____   _____

_____   _____

12. Define *righteousness*: _____

_____

41

The Church Worker: Her Responsibilities

JAMES 1:21-25

INTRODUCTION:

It has been said that of the twenty-seven books of the New Testament, twenty-one of them are devoted to instructing Christians regarding their work. Many of our sacred hymns are written to inspire us to greater service. Examples: "Work for the Night is Coming," "To the Work," "We'll Work," "There's Room in the Kingdom", etc. We know of no better way to "tell it like it is" than to quote from an old Negro Spiritual: "You can't get to heaven in a rockin chair, cause the Lord don't allow no lazy folks there."

I. THE WORKER'S RESPONSIBILITY.

A. It is sometimes the contention of women in the church that their one and only responsibility is to their family. It is certainly true that they must be "keepers at home" (Titus 2:5), but their duties do not end there as can be seen by reading the rest of that same Scripture.

B. Phoebe was said to be a "servant of the church which is at Cenchrea" (Rom. 16:6). Priscilla, along with her husband, Aquila, was Paul's "helper in Christ Jesus" (Rom. 16:3). "Greet Mary, who bestowed much labor on us" (Rom. 16:6), etc.

   1. We do not know what specific duties Phoebe, Priscilla or Mary performed but we do know that they served the church in some capacity. Priscilla helped to teach Apollos "the way of the Lord more perfectly" (Acts 18:26).

C. Many of us are guilty of using lack of time as an excuse for not doing more for the Lord. The same Lord who commanded that we work in the vineyard also originated time and set it in motion. He furnished us with all the time we need to do all He requires of us. We must organize our time so that we have enough to work for Him.

D. It is the God-given responsibility of every woman to provide the necessities of her family. "If *any* provide not for his own, and specially for those of his own house, he hath denied the faith, and is worse than an infidel" (I Tim. 5:8). Contrary to popular belief, this Scripture is not restricted to heads of households.

E. It is also the God-given responsibility of every Christian to "do good unto all men" as we have opportunity (Gal. 6:10).

42

1. We would like to point out here that, unless the context of a Scripture demands males exclusively, any time the English masculine noun or pronoun (he, him, man, men, etc.) is used in the Bible, it is what is called "neuter gender" and includes both sexes. For example: "He that believeth and is baptized shall be saved" (Mark 16:16); ". . . Commit thou to faithful men who shall be able to teach others also" (2 Tim. 2:2); "Let every one of you lay by him in store. . ." (I Cor. 16:2).

   a. There are relatively few instances where the Greek aner is used (such as in I Tim. 2:12) which means males exclusively. Otherwise the Greek anthropos is used which means mankind as opposed to Divinity without regard to sex (W. E. Vine).

F. Only the mentally incompetent, the very sick, and the dead have no responsibility to work in the kingdom. As is suggested in the song, there is room for both the great and the small things you can do.

G. There is no work enjoined upon the church but that each member is to be a participant in so far as his ability and talent allows. Each member will account for himself, not for what the church collectively has done. His individual contribution is the thing he must be concerned with primarily.

II. SOME SPECIFIC WORKS (See Titus 3:1).

A. We will study the duties of the Bible teacher in a later lesson so we will not go into detail on that subject at this time. However, it is a foregone conclusion that every Christian must be a teacher, both in word and in deed, though not necessarily in a classroom.

B. Our culinary skills can serve well in helping the needy. "The poor you will always have with you," said Jesus (Matt. 26:11). All the things that we commonly refer to as domestic duties (sewing, cleaning, washing, ironing, etc.) are assets, not mere superficial feminine qualities. Those who are sick or otherwise incapacitated need these things and we can supply them.

C. The elders, preachers, and teachers are frequently in need of help in the office. Attendance records, filing, letter writing, and other office duties are important functions of the church. Mailing the bulletins, keeping the tract rack filled, keeping abreast of the sick, visiting the sick, caring for the aged, admonishing the unfaithful, and many other duties can be performed by women in the church.

D. Of course all things we do in the church must be under the oversight of the elders and we are not free to meet and organize some sort of "Ladies Aid Society." Nonetheless, we

43

can work collectively within the framework of the organization which God ordained. We may also work individually as our opportunities and abilities allow. A ladies Bible class is a collective effort and is an example of what can be done. Most elders would appreciate and consider any suggestions one may have along this line.

E. The best method for teaching the lost is through personal contact. We can invite our acquaintances into our homes for Bible classes. Those who cannot personally do the teaching can do the inviting. Some other Christian will be happy to do the teaching and the hostess will be extending hospitality at the same time her friend is learning.

F. We should make a special effort to meet and warmly greet each visitor to our servies. If there is anything that will encourage them to return, it is a warm welcome extended by members of the church. If you are too shy to speak to strangers, you must work to overcome that problem.

G. If we really made a concerted effort to reach the lost, we could contact every person in the community. Let's work on it! "Let Mary do it, she's so much better at it than I" will never get *your* work done. If Mary spent all her time and energy doing the Lord's work, *your* work would still be undone. "So then every one of us shall give account of *himself* to God" (Rom. 14:12). None of us have enough righteousness to loan any to others as is taught in the parable of the ten virgins. We can and must help each other, but we can no more work for another than we can believe for another. The destiny of our souls is contingent upon our working for the Master.

CONCLUSION:

"*Work* out your own salvation with fear and trembling" (Phil. 2:12). "Ye see then how that by *works* a man is justified, and not by faith only" (Jas. 2:24). "And I heard a voice from heaven saying unto me, Write, Blessed are the dead which die in the Lord from henceforth: Yea, saith the Spirit that they may rest from their *labours;* and their *works* do follow them" (Rev. 14:13).

EXERCISES FOR HOME STUDY AND CLASS DISCUSSION

1. Phoebe was a "—————— of the church which is at Cenchrea" (Rom. 16:1).

2. Mary "bestowed much —————— on us" (Rom. 16:6).

3. Priscilla was Paul's "—————— in Christ Jesus" (Rom. 16:3).

4. Titus was instructed to remind the brethren to "be ready unto _____ _____ _____" (Titus 3:1).

5. All work which God enjoined upon the church collectively requires the participation of each member. True _____ false _____.

6. Revelation 14:13 offers a marvelous promise to the faithful church worker. What is it? _____

7. When the masculine noun or pronoun is used in the Bible it most often means the male sex exclusively. True_____ False _____

8. Priscilla usurped authority over her husband when she helped to teach Apollos. True _____ False _____.

9. Women are not required to give of their means because Paul said, "Let every one of you lay by *him* in store. . ." (I Cor. 16:2). True _____ False _____

10. "Ye see then how that by _____ a man is justified, and not by faith only" (James 2:24).

11. Ladies may meet and form a "Ladies Aid Society" through which to do their work. True _____ False _____. Give reasons for your answer.

_____

_____

_____

12. When the admonition "Work out your own salvation" was given, the apostle was suggesting that each person may form his own scheme of redemption and then proceed to work his plan. True _____ False _____. (See Phil. 2:12.)

The Bible Teacher:
Her Qualifications and Knowledge
2 TIMOTHY 2:2

INTRODUCTION:

When the queen of Sheba heard of the great wealth and unparalled wisdom of King Solomon, she did not believe it. To test him, she traveled from her kingdom in southwestern Arabia to the domain of the great monarch. There she propounded questions and riddles to him, all of which he answered conclusively and wisely. When she had seen that his riches and wisdom far exceeded the fame of which she had heard, she made this observation: "The half was not told me" (I Kings 10:1-7). So it is with the inexhaustible wealth to be found in the pages of Holy Writ. Should all Christians begin today to tell of the unsearchable riches of Christ and continue doing so until death takes us from this earth, this statement would still be true: "The half has never yet been told."

I. **THE TEACHER'S QUALIFICATIONS.**

A. We are very adamant in our insistence that teachers in our secular schools be well qualified. We demand that they have degrees from accredited schools certifying that they have completed the requirements which qualify them for their work.

B. For some reason, totally unknown to me, some in the church seem to have the idea that a Bible class teacher's qualifications need not be as stringent or are less important.

C. We are not suggesting that the Bible class teacher must have a degree from some college or university before she is equipped to teach the Bible. We are, however, insisting that she be "certified" by God that she has met and is meeting certain requirements.

D. The subject matter is unequalled by any other; the objective is likewise inimitable. Why, then, do some minimize the teacher's qualifications?

E. The qualified teacher is·

1. A faithful Christian, not only in attendance but in every other aspect of life as well. The teacher who is absent nearly as often as she is present, whether or not her absence is justified, will not be effective in teaching her students the importance of attending the services of the church. The same is true in all other areas of life.

2. A dedicated student of the Scriptures. She will not only study and prepare herself to teach the lesson at hand,

but she will, to the best of her ability, anticipate questions and try to be prepared to answer them.

3. One who possesses the talent to express her thoughts in such a way that others can understand and learn. Some very knowledgeable people do not have the talent to convey their ideas to others. Others have the talent but do not use or develop it. Still others find it very difficult to teach a certain age group while being quite adept at teaching another one. We need to recognize this truth and work where we can best use our talents.

II. THE TEACHER'S KNOWLEDGE.

A. It is a well known fact that one cannot possibly teach that about which she knows little or nothing.

B. Knowledge is an inexhaustible storehouse from which we continually draw. We shall not reach a time in this life when we have no further need for knowledge, and it is a warped mind that has no desire to learn.

C. We must know the will of the Lord if we ever hope to teach it to others. This is true not only for the Bible class teacher, but also for all who are disciples of Christ.

D. It is necessary to know enough about word usage and sentence structure to "handle aright the word of truth" (2 Tim. 2:15). Words are the mechanism by which our thoughts are conveyed.

1. We once heard of a man who was teaching a teenage Bible class who defined the phrase, "wrest the scriptures" (cf. 2 Pet. 3:16) to mean laying the Bible on the shelf and "resting" it. This is a classic example of ignorance of word definitions. Certainly "wrest" and "rest" are pronounced alike (called a homonym) but they are as far apart as the poles in meaning and origin. We indict neither the sincerity nor the zeal of this teacher, but neither are substitutes for knowledge.

E. The teacher must know enough about her subject matter to explain it intelligently and factually. The proficient teacher will learn what the Bible does *not* teach as well as what it *does* teach regarding her subject.

1. Example: the subject of instrumental music in worship. The Bible *does* teach singing; it *does not* teach playing.

F. The Bible is exclusive and inclusive, explicit and implicit, leaving no room for doubt or human opinion. It is "profitable for teaching, for reproof, for correction, for instruction in righteousness, that the man of God may be complete, furnished unto every good work" (2 Tim. 3:16-17). Peter said God has given us "all things that pertain unto life and godliness, *through the knowledge of him* that hath called us to glory and virtue" (2 Pet. 1:3). It follows, then, that anything pertaining to religion that is not found in God's word does *not* pertain unto life and godliness.

CONCLUSION:

The well qualified Bible teacher is a great asset to the church. Christ is exemplified in her life and in her words and there is no greater compliment.

May God help us to be "teachers of good things" in word, in deed, and in all phases of life (See Col. 3:17; Titus 2:5).

EXERCISES FOR HOME STUDY AND CLASS DISCUSSION

1. There are three things listed in outline that the qualified teacher must be or possess. What are they?
   a. _____
   b. _____
   c. _____
2. Is it necessary for all faithful Christians to be teachers? _____ (See 2 Tim. 2:2.)
3. How has God given us "all things that pertain unto life and godliness? (2 Pet. 1:3) _____

   _____
4. Timothy was instructed to be an "_____ of the believer" (I Tim. 4:12).
5. James said, "Be ye _____ of the word and not hearers only" (James 1:22).
6. What is the result of the "hearers only?" _____
7. The manifold wisdom of God is "made known through the _____" (Eph. 3:10).
8. Is it important that we recognize what our teaching talents are and develop them? _____ Give reason for your answer.

   _____
9. Any Christian can effectively teach small children. True_____ False_____
10. Both talents and knowledge are gifts of God. True _____ False _____.

48

The Bible Teacher:
Her Example and Work

I TIMOTHY 4:12

INTRODUCTION:

As we learned in the previous lesson, it is the obligation of every Christian, according to his or her ability, to tell of the Christ. Not one soul will be saved without learning of God and the only way to learn is to be taught. "And they shall be all taught of God. Every man therefore that hath heard, and hath learned of the Father, cometh unto me" (Jno. 6:45). Who is to do the teaching? "And the things that thou hast heard of me among many witnesses, the same commit thou to faithful men, who shall be able to teach others also" (2 Tim. 2:2). The "faithful men" here refers to all faithful mankind, both male and female. Christians are the ones who believe and practice truth and they are necessarily obligated to teach it to others.

I. TEACHING BY EXAMPLE.

A. The following poem written by Edgar Guest entitled "Sermons We See" expresses our thought beautifully.

I'd rather see a sermon, than hear one any day,
I'd rather one should walk with me than merely show the way.
The eye's a better pupil, and more willing than the ear;
Fine counsel is confusing, but example's always clear;
And the best of all the preachers are the men who live their creeds.
For to see the good in action is what everybody needs.
I can soon learn how to do it if you'll let me see it done;
I can watch your hands in action but your tongue too fast may run.
And the lectures you deliver may be very wise and true;
But I'd rather get my lesson by observing what you do.
For I may misunderstand you and the high advice you give.
But there's no misunderstanding how you act and how you live.

B. One may possess all the knowledge it is possible for him to acquire; he may have a great gift of oratory, but if he does not practice what he preaches, it will avail nothing.

C. Whether we like it or not, we are teaching by example. Our influence, either for good or bad, is being felt.

D. Paul told Timothy to "be thou an example of the believers, in word, in conversation (manner of life), in charity, in spirit, in faith, in purity. . ." (I Tim. 4:12). He did not say, be an example *to* the believers (though this is certainly included),

49

but rather, "be an example *of* the believers;" that is, be an example of what you teach, or be "Christianity personified." Peter said Christ left us an example, "That ye should walk in his steps" (I Pet. 2:21). James adds, "Be ye doers of the word ..." (Jas. 1:22).

E. "To the intent that now unto the principalities and the powers in the heavenly places might be made known *through the church* the manifold wisdom of God" (Eph. 3:10 ASV). The church is a manifestation of the manifold (many-fold) wisdom of God and it is necessarily enjoined upon every member to be a manifestation or demonstration of that wisdom.

F. Some have not the talent to stand before a group and teach orally nor do they possess the ability to teach in writing. But all accountable persons can and must teach by example.

  1. We have a very dear friend who is illiterate, but he is one of the best teachers we know. His example and his influence is appreciated by all who know him. He in indeed a "walking sermon." We would not, however, expect him to teach in a classroom.

II. SOME SUGGESTIONS FOR CLASS TEACHERS.

A. Learn which age group you are best qualified to teach.

B. Get to know your students and their parents well. This will help you to give individual attention where it is most needed.

C. Be well prepared; know your subject well. If you are teaching the very young, understand that they have not the ability to concentrate on any one thing for a very long period of time—their attention and concentration span is very short.

D. Use visual aids when possible, especially with the young children. One retains much more of what he sees than he does of that which he hears.

E. Encourage class participation. Teach children to pray by asking them to lead the prayer in the classroom. Make the class as interesting as possible.

F. Be sure you have enough of the best possible material with which to work and learn to be proficient in its use.

G. Remember that the learning process is incomplete until the student has *learned*. Your teaching is only half the process. Repetition is necessary in many cases and review lessons are always helpful.

CONCLUSION:

We understand that women are somewhat restricted by God in teaching the Bible. They may never, at any time nor in any place, "teach nor usurp authority *over the man*" (I Tim. 2:12). Contrary to what some say about this passage, an investigation of the text will show beyond any doubt that it is not confined to a Bible class or a

50

meeting house where the church meets, but is of universal application. Incidentally, this has *always* been God's law. On the other hand, aged women are commanded to teach and only restriction to time and place is found in the above reference. (See Titus 2:3-5.)

The story is told of a convention where there were both experienced and inexperienced speakers. One famous orator in beautiful voice and perfect diction quoted the 23rd Psalm. The following speaker was very inexperienced and he had also planned to quote the same Psalm. Falteringly, he began speaking in an almost inaudible voice. Soon, however, he forgot his audience and began speaking to the Shepherd of whom David had written. At the end of his "speech", instead of the usual applause there was a hush over the audience. The first speaker rose slowly to his feet and said, "I apologize for my 'drama'. You see, I knew the 23rd Psalm well, but this man knows the Shepherd."

Let's all get to know the Shepherd, then we will be able to tell of Him to others.

EXERCISES FOR HOME STUDY AND CLASS DISCUSSION

1. What does the word "conversation" as used in I Tim. 4:12 mean?
   _____

2. Since women may teach a class of children or women, she may also preach or teach in a mixed assembly. True _____ False _____

3. In what way are women restricted in their teaching? _____
   _____

4. Does the scripture found in I Tim. 2:12 apply at all times or while in the meeting house of class room only? _____
   Prove your answer. _____
   _____

5. Women are commanded to teach. True _____ False _____.

6. Is it possible for woman to teach a man without teaching "*over* the man" (See Acts 18:26.) _____ How may this privilege be abused?
   _____

7. Was there ever a time when woman had the God-given right to teach or usurp authority over the man? _____

8. In the Old Testament we learn that Deborah was a judge of Israel. Was this by God's appointment and if so, was it in contradiction to

His law stated in I Tim. 2:12; Gen. 3:16, et. al.? See Judges 4 and 5.

_____

_____

_____

9. Paul said faithful men "shall be able to teach others." Thus, all faithful Christians are able to teach in class rooms. True————— False—————.

10. We must conduct our lives to personify Christianity before we can hope to teach by word of mouth. True————— False —————.

The Citizen:
Subjection to Civil Government

ROMANS 13:1-7

INTRODUCTION:

We are privileged to live in the most wonderful nation upon the earth. Whereas it is not a "Christian nation," per se, it is founded upon faith in God and belief in individual rights.

America is unique in many ways, not the least of which is that we are a self-governing democracy. It has been stated that "America is Americans attempting self-government while situated in a fortunate geographical position." We are by far the most progressive, the most prosperous and the most promising of all nations, Russian propaganda to the contrary, notwithstanding.

I am proud of my American heritage and thankful to God and my forefathers for having made it possible. I resent a mob of "rabble-rousers" who seek to disrupt and destroy the government, having nothing in mind that even equals it, much less to improve it.

I. CIVIL GOVERNMENT IS ORDAINED OF GOD (Rom. 13:1-7).

A. We know that all political incumbents are not God-fearing men. That is not what the text teaches. Their *position* of authority is ordained of God and they have not only the right but also the obligation to enact and enforce laws for the good of the citizenry.

B. Some may say, "Because the authorities are corrupt and unjust, I have no responsibility to them."

1. Jesus and the apostles lived during a literal "reign of terror." History teaches that the Roman government under the power of the Caesars was the most corrupt ever known and yet the New Testament, with its admonition to "be subject unto the higher powers," was written during that very period.

2. Jesus Himself, while possessing the apex of authority, subjected Himself to civil rulers, corrupt as they were. Who, then, are we to say we have no obligation to obey them? Jesus told Pilate, "You have no power but that which has been given from above" (Jno. 19:10-12).

3. Can you imagine Jesus, followed by the Twelve, marching on Rome carrying placards and demanding that they be heard? Peter said He left us an example that we should walk in his steps and he did not leave any such example!

4. This does not mean that we should complacently "go along" with every thing and not use our civil rights through established process of law or that we should not

53

attempt to correct that which is amiss in government. Fortunately we live in a democracy where we have the privilege of selecting those whom we feel will best serve the public. This is not to be done by burning bodies, lying in the streets, malicious backbiting, irreverence for the flag, or any other undignified means that so-called social reformers may concoct.

C. "Submit yourselves to every ordinance of man for the Lord's sake; whether it be to the king, as supreme; or unto governors, as unto them that are sent by him for the punishment of evildoers, and for the praise of them that do well. For so is the will of God, that with well doing ye may put to silence the ignorance of foolish men" (I Peter 2:13-15).

D. "Whosoever therefore resisteth the (civil) power, resisteth the ordinance of God: and they that resist shall receive to themselves damnation" (Rom. 13:2).

II. WHY BE SUBJECT TO CIVIL AUTHORITIES.

A. All the power that authorities have was given to them by God. "For there is no power but of God: the powers that be are ordained of God" (Rom. 13:1b). All things that God has ever done for mankind have been for the good of mankind.

B. Everything in heaven and on earth is sustained by law, either natural, divine, or civil. One second without natural law would destroy the universe, for it is by that law that nature subsists. One second without divine law would result in universal spiritual death, for it is by that law that spiritual life is sustained. Likewise, a very short period of time without civil law would effect devastation such as has never been witnessed, for it is by that law that our rights and privileges are preserved.

1. For example, imagine Big City, U.S.A. at 5 P.M. on Friday. There are no traffic signals, no road warnings, no police directing traffic, etc. How many people would get home from work safely?

2. This is but one seemingly small item of the civil law and yet we can see the results would be disastrous.

C. The omniscient God knew that many would walk in the counsel of the ungodly, some would have no regard for the rights and possessions of others, that there would be thieves, murders, whoremongers, and such like. Since it was not in His plan to personally, physically punish the evildoers or protect the innocent, it was necessary to establish an institution to serve that purpose. The civil government is that organization.

CONCLUSION:

We have everything to gain and nothing to lose by submitting ourselves to civil rulers and it is impossible to obey God without so doing.

EXERCISES FOR HOME STUDY AND CLASS DISCUSSION

1. To obey God one must obey the laws of the land. True ——————
   False ——————.
2. Are there any Biblical restrictions placed upon civil authorities?
   ——————(see Acts 5:29).
3. Are we justified in defying authorities who are corrupt?_____
4. Peter said that kings and governors are sent by —————— for the punishment of evildoers (I Peter 2:13-15).
5. The Bible teaches that all political incumbents are God-fearing men. True—————— False——————.
6. Jesus told Pilate, "Thou couldest have no power at all against me except it be given thee —————— ——————" (John 19:11).
7. Everything in heaven and on earth is sustained by law. True —————— False ——————.
8. Name the three categories of law and how they affect us.
   a. ———————————————————————————————
   b. ———————————————————————————————
   c. ———————————————————————————————
9. A prime example of submission to civil authorities is Jesus Himself. What would our status be had He not been subject to Jewish and Roman authorities? Explain your answer in your own words.

   ———————————————————————————————

   ———————————————————————————————

   ———————————————————————————————

   (See Heb. 9:22-28; I Cor. 15:3.)
10. Jesus could have called for "legions of angels" to resist His arrest in the garden. Why did He choose not to do that?

   ———————————————————————————————

The Citizen's Allegiance
TITUS 3:1

INTRODUCTION:

God charges each individual with a responsiblity to be a good, law-abiding citizen wherever his or her citizenship happens to be. Being a citizen of the United States does not lessen the obligation, but it does make it easier to fulfill.

There is one area wherein God has restricted the authority of civil governments and that is where civil statutes conflict with His law (cf. Acts 5:29). God's authority is always supreme and there is none that annuls it.

I. HOW MAY WE BE GOOD CITIZENS?

A. Obedience to the laws of the land is only one area wherein our civil allegiance lies.

B. We need to be informed citizens. Certainly if we do not know the law, the issues, or the problems, we can do little to help. How many times have you gone to the election polls and looked bewilderingly at a ballot full of unrecognizable names and issues? An "eeny, meny, miney, moe" method of voting will scarcely get the desired candidate elected or the issue passed or defeated that will best serve the county, state or country.

C. We all want our freedom to continue and we are convinced that all candidates are not patriotic servants who respect our Bill of Rights. Some are egotistical bigots whose sole purpose is to satisfy their own selfish desires.

D. Admittedly, it is very difficult to select the best candidate. Lies seem to be an integral part of political strategy and many politicians are master liars. This is indeed a very sad state of affairs and is certainly one area that needs vast reform. Such men need to be exposed and deposed.

　1. Just prior to the 1972 Presidential election, Brother Frank Puckett said, "If the Presidential candidates are actually guilty of just half of that with which their opponent charges them, both men should be in the penitentiary."

E. Let us diligently attempt to sort the good from the bad and do our best to elect the best person for the job. Those who do not exercise their privilege to vote have no right to complain that the wrong person is in office.

F. God has charged each person with the obligation to do his best in whatever endeavor he is involved. Mr. Lincoln, in his very famous Gettysburg Address, said our government was "conceived in liberty and dedicated to the proposition that all men are created equal." We want to help keep it that way by participating as best we can in it's affairs.

G. We are prone to complain about the school activities or policies but do little more than complain. Most of us are not qualified to tell school administrators how to run the schools, but we need not sit idly by while immoral activities or unjust policies are practiced in the public schools. We are citizens in our school districts and, as such, have the prerogative of being heard by the school board and other administrators.

H. Local law enforcement agencies often request the assistance of its citizens in some particular effort. We may have the opportunity to help in such cases.

1. By being law-abiding ourselves, we are a constant source of help.

2. Some time ago we saw a sign with the picture of a policeman on it which read: "If you think we're pigs, next time you're in trouble, call a hippy."

3. Do not be the kind of person who does not want to be involved. The very fact that you are a citizen involves you.

4. Call to the attention of law enforcement agencies all known law breakers. How much better our communities would be if every citizen reported those whom they know to be involved in illegal practices. God does not ignore law (covenant) breakers and warns against them (Rom. 1:31).

5. Law enforcement officials are to be respected and obeyed. They serve as ministers of God for good (Rom. 13:4). They may not always be just and impartial but that does not lessen their authority. We may report them to the proper authorities if we see them practice partiality or dishonesty, but obey them, we must!

II. PAYING TAXES.

A. The Pharsees, who totally misunderstood the nature of Jesus' mission, thought He was a political rival of Caesar. Thinking to "entangle him in his words" they asked Him, "Is it lawful to give tribute to Caesar, or not?" He answered them by asking whose inscription was on the tribute money. "They say unto him, Caesar's. Then saith he unto them, render therefore unto Caesar the things which are Caesar's; and unto God the things that are God's" (Matt. 22:15-22). Let us remember that this was Tiberius Caesar under whom the infamous Pontius Pilate served and who was emperor when our Lord was crucifed. Jesus did not way, "you don't have to pay any taxes until this corrupt government is straightened out!"

B. The great amount of tax money that is being literally given away to ne'er-do-wells who have never worked in their lives and have no intention of working to earn anything in the future is a constant source of irritation to us. However, one of the very wonderful attributes of this nation is that there can be no taxation without representation. Therefore, we are represented in the government by those who have a voice in the employment of our tax dollars and we may state our opposition to or approval of the use of our taxes to our representative. Should enough of us state our opposition to the many give-away programs, they would soon cease. Nonetheless, the fact that our taxes may not be used wisely does not give us license to refuse to pay them.

C. We must provide things honest in the sight of all men (Rom. 12:17). Cheating on tax forms is dishonest and inexcusable. Failure to report all taxable income or padding deductions is both lying and stealing. Getting caught by the Internal Revenue Service is not the only danger; one who practices such things has already been "caught" by God and will suffer the consequences if repentance is not forthcoming.

CONCLUSION:

We suggest that a diligent study be made of Romans 13:1-8, I Peter 2:13-17, and Titus 3:1. Let us remember that one cannot be an acceptable citizen of the kingdom of heaven without being a good citizen of society. The precious promises of God are for those who serve Him in all walks of life.

"For rulers are not a terror to good works, but to the evil. Wilt thou then not be afraid of the power? Do that which is good, and thou shalt have praise of the same" (Romans 13:3).

EXERCISES FOR STUDY AND CLASS DISCUSSION

1. ——————— ——————— was emperor at the time Christ was crucified.

2. It is not wrong to drive 40 mph in a 35 mph zone if there is no policeman near. True ——— False ———.

3. Most of us are not qualified to "run" the schools, therefore we have no voice in their policies. True ——— False ———.

4. Christians have the right to appeal to civil authorities. (See Acts 25:10-11.) True——— False ———.

5. We may withhold taxes that might be used by corrupt men for evil purposes. True ——— False ———.

6. The Christian must ignore law breakers and not involve himself in community affairs. True ——— False ———.

7. Paul said, "Rulers are not a ——————— to good works, but to the evil" (Rom. 13:3).

8. Peter said, "Submit yourselves to every ordinance of man for the ——————— sake" (I Pet. 2:13).

9. Governors are sent by God "for the ——————— of evildoers, and for the ——————— of them that do well" (I Pet. 2:14).

10. List some ways in which each Christian may be a good citizen and be helpful rather than a hindrance.

———————————————————————————

———————————————————————————

———————————————————————————

———————————————————————————

———————————————————————————

—Notes—

—Notes—

—Notes—

—Notes—

—Notes—

www.ingramcontent.com/pod-product-compliance
Lightning Source LLC
Chambersburg PA
CBHW071931020426
42331CB00010B/2811